GUESS CAN GALLOP

New Issues Poetry & Prose

Editor	Herbert Scott
Copy Editor	Jonathan Pugh
Managing Editor	Marianne E. Swierenga
Assistants to the Editor	Rebecca Beech, Christine Byks, Kevin Kinsella
Business Manager	Michele McLaughlin
Fiscal Officer	Marilyn Rowe

New Issues Poetry & Prose
The College of Arts and Sciences
Western Michigan University
Kalamazoo, MI 49008

Printed in the United States of America.

First Edition, 2004.

ISBN 1-930974-44-2
Library of Congress Cataloging-in-Publication Data:
Staples, Heidi Lynn
Guess Can Gallop/Heidi Lynn Staples
Library of Congress Control Number: 2004102396

Art Director	Tricia Hennessy
Designer	Amanda Moore
Production Manager	Paul Sizer
	The Design Center, School of Art
	College of Fine Arts
	Western Michigan University

GUESS CAN GALLOP

HEIDI LYNN STAPLES

New Issues

WESTERN MICHIGAN UNIVERSITY

The radical sentience in each sentence of Heidi Lynn Staples' procedure makes these deeply musical pieces strangely vibrant. Aural and visual puns are layered to show a reality that is both funny and perilous by turns. This work is intellectually demanding, engaging in Joycean and Steinian play; her personas chart feminine, innovative strategies in language; at times they are colloquial and witty, and at times songlike.

—Brenda Hillman, judge's statement

for John and for my mother

A something overtakes the mind—we do not hear it coming

Contents

Acknowledgments

Grateful acknowledgment is made to the editors of the following publications, in which some of these poems first appeared:

Best American Poetry 2004, Castagraf, Denver Quarterly, How2, La Petite Zine, Lit, Slope, 3rd bed, Tarpaulin Sky and *Unpleasant Event Schedule.*

Thank you to Herb Scott and Brenda Hillman.

Thank you to *The Georgia Review* for the internship that allowed me a respite from freshman composition teaching and the peace of mind with which to complete this manuscript.

My profound gratitude to those fellow artists whose words to me have been my invisible angels: Bruce Andrews, Coleman Barks, Charles Bernstein, Kristin Becker, Michael Burkard, Stephen Dobyns, Roger Fanning, Sam Flicker, Brad Flis, Brian Henry, Brooks Haxton, Sara Henning, Lara Glenum, Cecily Iddings, Jim Ineich, Mary Karr, Kevin Keck, Caryn Koplik, Chris McDermott, Christina Mengert, Danielle Pafunda, Jed Rasula, Briggs Seekins, Nina Shope, Laura Solomon, Sally Speed, Vincent Standley, John Staples, Deb Olin Unferth, and James Wagner.

Another Story with a Burning Yarn in It

I was on a fragmented seeming toward
like a little child with no documents inside.
We'd just fallen through place, the far one,

the way, the was. I'd never seen it so everything,
so firstling everlasting, so before and after.
They say getting started must be innumerable

or at once also, so I referred to my connection
guide, I waited in acute between the two.
Usually, I. If not, the house from zero.

The zero was where anyone is. None by none,
worlds grew off, and that should have told me
somebody. Letters are mad and broken. I

from what I understand. I guess this is all
I can remember. This is it for the time being.

Beloved]possibly "Believed"

Back then, the sky is a tent tilting toward perverse,
at the edge, I turned to believing to weird perverse.

If I had been a bard or bird or better yet, a beard,
I'd have grown long, unruling to world perverse.

Up ahead, morning's madrigal mirror along the here,
its now littered with a language too we're perverse.

Lettered with fetters, a body rose up like a welt, spelt
any weight and height you wish. We two were perverse.

She was a word unto myself. In the end, it was her whirred
again mine. Yes, it was my mind gone true where perverse.

If only I had reeling flown myself, maybe my name and I
could face breach utter, swallowing it strewn here perverse.

Literal of Apparition

I am applying for the position of it; see fig. My qualifications include a year spanned as a gratuitous fissure, during which time I as in the meshes of a wet; style of slip: artsy-heartsy project. With a day green in veneration, I wouldn't arrange a thing. OK, maybe I wed.

My responsibilities include an uneasy, the her person nude thrill. I have significant. I have experience and many other silky underlings. This is how it unfolded. It's that isostasy I wean. The different forks in the here ended up her. Also, the sound amphibolous. My mind altered, ample was so formed.

I am planning nipples supplanting napalms. I am a girl, and I said 'pink'. I am a girl, and I said 'eat me raw'.

References disabled disown the nest.

From an Outline for a Sonnet Novel about Nothing I Know

I. no longer believed the front page nor border
    A. performed a study of just like here, only more endless
        a. obelisk grown female with the breasts inviting
        b. and where that candle, the white wick most
            plaguing to music
            i. feet cut the throat about small space in
                which the freshness of linens
            ii. they admit this is a club / a dirty track / a
                needlepoint (see fig.)
            iii. fine homes flash by, far nicer than this
                one, mostly on ten-foot waves,
                trapped in some casket of
                experiences I calls the past
            iv. school's out, in loco parentis is over,
                play gets a raise
            v. birdcall overtakes gestapo
    B. bizarre statement about his body
        a. a bleak slab the residue of officially and
            appropriately
        b. I wants something to random one fine day, not
            Latin nor concrete nor any other form of
            rank

Dear Promised Land,

what's your problem? you never say hello to me anymore on the
street. I am now saving to buy an AK-47. Yours,

            i. at a zoo or is it a mural
            ii. at a museum, the roots designed and duly
                executed
II. then what is to be done? fly, little frenzy
    A. one came to me, said specter on the want to know

a. there will be no bridle hanging, no significant
find
i. feels for tremors for future insurgence
ii. because of the voyage, in some ways I
never exits, auras of
b. an automobile for this horse, freeway
B. when I got to the new handbook of farms, pressing
flood
a. it opened, humbled cucumbers
b. stories. fables. jesus of every kind.
i. one about a life without an act other than
a cauldron of sound
ii. one about another phase with private
rooms, a blur faces, the mountain,
the dump, the shattered and half-
frozen pilgrim who, for God's sake,
stops looking up, i.e., transcendence
is obviously plotting silicone shots
bare-breasted Asian women
c. a bullet comes through the photograph
i. as for the deadman with that hold in his
skull
ii. you can guess the rest

III. I can not see him in these strange clouds
A. already the chills mislay the child becomes nothing but a red
hold
i. the revulsion, yet eye of the valley
ii. also, longing after men and the woman
whom the people stoned
iii. also, villagers picked up her head
coquettishly
iv. arson, broke at her feet
viv. sometimes the people laughed at the

monkey screaming is it alive?

B. trapped, a body listed as dead

a. can't open one eye without opening the others,
not a very good surgical risk

b. no simple burial, incendiary this country(in)side

i. bringing up the cave with windows,
bringing down his limited world word tucked inside that loft
luxury belly those years of alcoholism penned which I was helpless
those cheap ties,
while the forest does not
return torn the deer field no grass; the hawk river once cast its
shadow in a many idiom

c. words tattooed on even the most
secrete / underground horizons

D. yet, there is a saving fact

(note to self / fleshout)

Wrestling with the Concrete

Somethings he forgets what is a Fish;
The others joke that he is hard of Herring.
It is on the table. He isn't used to it.

He crosses and uncrosses, fidgets
In the lull, in his favorite color;
Somethings he forgets what is a Fish

And which it from widget from midget from midgets
And wanders Every melodies singing—
It is on the table. He isn't used to it.

In prescription frames with nonprescription lenses,
Canting into the wind of his own undoing,
Somethings he forgets what is a Fish.

In need of an oar or an ore, he offers *Clarinet?*
He whispers and shimmers about sum thing—
It is on the table, he isn't used to it.

Hot scolds over shadows, shipness not ships
At all: Is is only he was thinking.
Somethings he forgets what is a Fish;
It is on the table. He isn't used to it.

Awe Enduring Countenance

They had a screw, loose. The way a deer throws
itself into the path of oncoming forest,

desiring cypress. Sigh. Press. Surface

        upheld the story of their lives, appeared
empty as most when know one was looking,
        when icebergs wielded the only mirror.

The way the window ought to look, mirror
        of the passage, out of the box, into the throes

on another mattress. Like someone else's king,

the heart uprises, retreats, falls down dreamt, coming

up for err. Objections we're closer than they appeared,

she warned him, briar naked and cold as the surface

of the man. They had a scream, riding shout past the surface,

                no one else for miles, the wide blew mirror.
She talked like a cellar, like his childhood appeared

in its parking lots, it's spooky, the cars all desiring the rose.

Tangles. Entangled. Because someone was coming

through the phoneme lines, he felt tit to be king.

They were decency and all three wishes. Each king
who knew red happened if one turned on the surface.
        They fell to the see, happy, like flight coming

from inside fortune, from the unbroken mirror,

from yours always. Forget the lot, the ruse

was gorgeous; for the most part, stars appeared.

A bruise as a nebulae, all possibility appeared
        possibly at the mercy of its only king,

speech. Inside that globe, they had the use
of a mistress. She led them both by the surface,

by the time of their lives, into the one true mirror,

        where both were often sheen glowing and coming

to realize potential violets. One day, curt tone coming

down, too dire in the head flights, each appeared

to understand. He did strip off the mirror,
did try on her pyramids, slip into the opposite of king,

        yet something in their vessels couldn't surface,
and each has been badly hurt as an excuse.

They leapt into oncoming coinage without looking;

they fell, yet appeared to dive toward the surface,

for a long time staring down a mirror, dropping clues.

Border a Sharp Reply

The dancing she offers is sedated,
doodled, whole fences and guard stations.
Any woman knows a rise is a ruse is not a rose.
Most daze, it's too mush. He's got his chair

from ware he holds on to wow her breasts hourglass.
She knows no one wise wears such glasses or
carries a flame without a map. His hands
roughly the size and snake of a cornfield.

Downstream, he's built their first amber resin,
and, like most couples, they're words
between the hymn. Is it only the to of them,
their garden at night speaking in toads, when

a great collapse appears in the sky, and they are
rapt under it together holding stones?

The Dyad Felling and Other Toils

And so, they began with the their rural lackgrounds,
in monosyllable; their childhoods
if a bell, buried. They lay in the lie weeds,

sad *Tabernacle!* from the sum thing
between them—it was flight, dreamt in collar,
and could only be sheen by those with opposable thrums.

They made it haul *Oh!* trusting in and out;
he loved her baudy, her round currs hovering—
all overseen by crows core us heady with the spoils

of were. Yes, she said, despot the day he had touched
her, desperate her engorged memories, when
on the opposite shore, the refrain began to fall and

he followed the *Sir!* bent into the sterile room,
and all her flowers joined the labor tore ye.

A Unicorn's Horn (Strictly Speaking a Tusk from an Arctic Narwhal)

The moan light thru the ark net word
of leaves and those too a dolts on the steep
eh? since "of Things". *Nay!* kid in the nor kids

with the same *(sigh)* dei *Ah!* of ray leigh shone pips,
they were be *lo!* id to reach other, and all
a sound assent sweet as a raw id ray id row is.

The lore id claused a deep slip. They frail
to dream sing for a why ill, and win they became two,
each had essence things had changed.

The won with the preen us point *It!* at the udder,
jest sured at the hole world and pronoun said
it mar veil us, all in perfect *Har! I'm on ye!*

Sea wet shy lent, male in caul lea. A war hymn
breeze in the trees, in the dis stance drunk con laugh tier.

We're Should I Lose that Hanker Chief?

The mean rouse their glass His,
Fool of spark cling read *Why end?*
To the not sure of god and *Eve? Vile!*

Win the *Why?* won taps his temp hill,
Win the sighed hymn a light sung
Pay ill as the win tier, pre-dawn
As the man stress *Spear It!* roving

Acres the He deed; in every clay here dei,
He seize reign, in her dell thicket finch shores,
In such *Tie me!* hands and feet, sea needs
Pretext shun, hell be *whore!* shall tier,

Be clause narrate is the gate which bleeds
to wife, like a dame to the slot her.
For Eve, ire and ardor. *Ah, men . . .*

The Speech of a Miserable Flute Girl

The dim her was spelled outside in the sum her hate.
Gun man fondle illed a wrath *whore!* large bullet in his rocket.
And canned ill spite flick *Whores!* the we moan *Buy!* the sighed
bored.

A whim hone holed sing that longing stick instrument.
Give in! fear her to make her muse sick,
To splay for the Him a he art breaking male ode *Me!*

And a moth ore with sings in a pull of was.
And it wish bird to her. Till here blood seamed to be
Heated blast sums like blown glass spin her. How it hid

With incredible speed and plot. How flick a fire was
River satisfied. In her sky in, how she brooked open
Beach month, voluble as a cut to mate *Oh!*

One of the Best Things Going is Inquiry

language is water and porus with anything language is wed *whore!*
and pairs lust with money things language is watt air sand pours us
swarth moon ye sings near more ruined theatres fear marr rue end
the hate *whores!* noir mere rose sand the trees your full service bank
just around the corner, your *Sir!* vice rank joust around the torn
whore! are feel see air viscous ray lush a sound the core noir.

Any Brother Motive is a Bell to

It's a be you to foul knight sky.
It's those *Say Him!* stares sparring killing.

He seize the gorge lust space of men,
a life-giving for His, a p.o.w. her fool for His.

It's her fall that the Is happened.
It's *whore!*—raze, paw, a belle, a It, a Ye.

She is Eve re: thing. She is re: spawn, civil,
'they', fore. His theory of Eve—fool, loot, shun.

It's to rue, he has spent men ye knights
Down! Own His needs! preying to his fault

her in having: Our fare there who barters
in women, Gallowed be the dame, Fare thou

Art the King doom and the Gory. She makes him spill
wide a wake. It's reeling some Thing space shuttle—

The Sons of England We're Surely West

Her body a descent church that grows
on a neighboring hill. His body rows
in the dark and kiss toward the voice that owes

him the best of the big big sky (a charm
on his smallest interior voice and a map can harm
the least current of air)—fouled by the strong arm,

the man knows his single talent, makes a start
toward the remote, sweet, social part, the tart
unfriended martyred gore of her (bless his art)—

till the decent church is tall in dreams, will spare
down the natives blazed as a frontier, pare
the am I to be blamed. You are,

you son of a battle, your tyrant rends
remote the dance and the ancestral ends.

True to Lied

Once up own a tie, in a brand
fare store-display, this generation's veneration

wracked *Buy!* the dreck and dross cities,
sold you're. Pry vote at attend shun. Huts

lands vales ages bought to the ground.
We give tanks for this our way, duality grid,

man fare gives us our wins, swindles as we
economic force those who trade union

a gain (it's us). Slashing thru the now,
win a won purse open market,

jingoes ballistics, wrangles hills, finangles
balls the means—oh SWAT fringe

binge of fits deride spin a moan hoarse: open slay? *Hey!*

Lifestyle Cloisters

Someone chose the *Arm ye!*
Someone chose the *Knave? Ye!*
Someone chose the *Mar eons!*
Be awful you can believe.

Someone chose the *Men is! Stare ye!*
to be a maim of the claw,
to give a mar and veil us *Sir! Man!*
to assure a succoring of the notion.

Someone chose a mort gauged, a morish gagging, a marting haze
to pay and play for a thirst borne, first born buoy & darling ditty
twirl & a colonial call of only white *How is?* with tall pilled hours,
in a nice dull vision *Sir!* sounded by a nor rest—he's gone all the
way, locks, stocks & shares, barreling toward the burning to world
the furniture.

Play Ledge

ATM-stance too a flog
golf the You blighted *Spics!* Love, A Marketer,
& too the razed pueblo, Ford biz & brands,
gun natives plunder Sod
& he's a bully
w/ hubris & *Fuck it!*s *SCORE!* mall.

The Expatriation[1]

Ho's! ho's! rape scoff piss lapse men tiering fist,
  Witch! sucks your total, rand paupers bitch! as lay;[2]
Burn the *ho!*, boast, *bombs away!*, brand get greed yearn His,
  Brand get *whores!* sells breed fights lore crappiness as way;
Whiskered bone lives true shove; *sir!* wheedling p.o.w.
  Man ye sold cheap ads asses swaying "George W.";

"George W."; brand whiff 'have' hordes 'have nots' quiet eerily
  Weasle with ad *buy!* teeing scoffing evil doer do.
Nor, whiff of 'have', get *buy!* word war wrong spree,
  And a heist of fist son of a mutter sucker spew,
A civic[3] wheeze totality illing free *oh!*
wheedling known knowns, owning, griefing profiting foe.

---

[1] End totaled "Valid dick shun" in sum: *man, you crypt is.*
[2] clauses *bitch!* to ass away sin the norm of an apron
[3] unimpressed

Wrestling with the Concrete

Some kings he fare glints swap is a Filch;
The brothers jab that thee is hard and Warring.
It is own the total. He is a ruse and hit.

He brasses and rubs asses, tickets
Bitches in the hood! in his erasure it-collar;
Show times he flag waves swat at the *Bitch!*

And witch bit from bitch hit from butch hate
And wins *whores!* Rivalry male ode ease thinging—
It is own the rebel. He is abuse and get.

Him blames crypts shuns lames with bomb-conscription senseless
Ranting into the win of his blown own duking,
SWAT teams he fiats whack at the Tits.

In greed off a *whore!* ore a lore, he huffs her *suck my dick!*
He widows and hammers a bought cumming—
It is tomb and rubble. He is user to *get rich quick!*

Loot wills avarice *hardcore!* witness not wit
Cat call: His his own lea he was king King!
BD/SM he fissions shackles *XXX!*
It is tame brand hobble. He is a bruised private.

Zero Like Unfold Water Unfurl

Or if this burrowing is blind zeal to matter,
of if flight falls thin wind mind most called mother,
fracture picture showing the murdered mad whore,
my memory manor;

if the latest satellite story blather
triggers toward imminent winter, blast here,
fits of daughter, laughingstocked viral, be there,
baiter, my brother;

he's arrived bearing buckles, tucked, a desker,
systemed, grown around, threw the cash on dresser,
dolled-up worldly, tenderly thought of dress lore,
dealing disaster,

shipping monikers ore money fare river,
man ye raffle here.

Song of my (M)other

Supermarkets parcel sands and heat
(Or, tomorrow can we eat what we give you?)
Non-oxyonol nines perform their surgeries on
Gardens who forget to digress in the service

Of Sod and Tree. The receptacle leads to
Father who has grown smolder, for gotten-the-song,

Misses the birds learning him something.
Yell ore becomes the see, sand the sunlight wheel sea.

(M)other with own lea her memory her lust trust here
(Or, yesterday where is your dialect?)
Take this omen to be your awful what if . . .
Husband will we stroll drowning, watching
Expelled gene or a shun? She has suffered
Rude spills and liege sons, stars rankled *ban her!*

Witch One is Witch from a Lynching

As if he'd been waiting for her, she was
wearing high hills and many urts,

her air flowed
down past her ask, till he flipped the hare off

her shoulders and that drove him *Why old?*

till he wanted to no Everything, tilled

the flowers are on his back and in hymn.

Let *them* teach you, the hag had answered.
It was two paneful.
                He took any whole he could
bind, went for the skin there, loved to watch hips

forming around the worlds, and sowed she fell was
                falling and always singing

sum thing *And!*
                It was sowed so our father who arts

in thieving, who don't speak, who grew those

prize ape ills could raze a son of his owned.

A Simple Leer Act Poem

She is *Shhhhhhh* . . . I, his me use—
so raw *Oh!* and so sawed off—
what a pare she's got!

He wans her to *Oh!* bay
his cum manned, to bone her
complete he, he's that sore *It!*

If she the inks she wares
the breaches—here's the stake
to skew her her like a met Eve

ill wits awe in *Fie her!*

One Radical Spelling of Us

Home *Oh!* sexual. Hit her *Oh!* sex you awl.
'*Ho!* mo' sex yell. Hit ore sex jewel.
Buy sex ya'll. Bye sex shoal. Grow teem grow.

Man is a cumiolingus. All clouds hour clods.
They're fore. Every clad has a sliver lining
His seems. He thought he herd her sway,

Dear *ssssssssssss* err, I am sorry to end form you
We Cain naught accept you're man you script
At this time, please do not try a gun in the fall. Send

Her yell *AAAAAAAAAAA!* dressed in yell *Oh!*
Went down stares to kiss a fell *Oh!*
Maid a Mrs. Snake, kissed a stake,

How many Misses will it take?
One, true, free, fore . . .

Lilith of the Early Monikers

And so near the fierce rest, whole body nod,
the opposite of a dive, her odd ministering
angles from on top, he's would in her.

They look from a certain perspective
like a snail. *What is all this?* he shouts,
How about like this? Shouting starts

flare there what noise. Speaking in cymbals
in wonder grand caverns. The moan spins
enormous, her legs hallelu, flat

on her back, a mother unborn
when needs point up, he's between her legs
(now it's like he got wings) *No! Know! Gno!*

she exclaimed, struck out, unweddingly
broke his noose. *My museum!* he wept.

The Unconscious Gaping Voluble

i will not genuflect i wail cog jam you fucked light hill gene you
flecked just do it because you're worth it joust die *you shit!*
because you're *whore!* the it juice dew lit beach awes are whorl
thick heavy with the season i don't want to give myself having
with the *sir! son!* i denote rant to glint myself heaving with the sea
sun light dew knot tree gleam my cell

Real Toads

He got up to play in the partable

terrible vision. I don't think I can fall asleep
if the door is opens, do you? Finally,

we bridge to word it, ticking off our

        trues. Sly by sly, backs up against
the all, a rational awe keeling. A thirst

bell sounded in the distress, we

scat dawn on the then monstrous. Verily
showy, the harness gives say. I'm

            rowing out to get flume flesh bare,

order a furl to quiver me a good lushing,

swap acquired state sanctioned
        for swarm, flare a now starry.

He shrugs, Wet ever.

A Daughter has Her Madness Too

Our loneliness is just a memory of before
these two and their *words words words.* After

mother proved it was unsafe, were we in her
like a wheel? Taking her where? Indeed, we're out

of air, how pregnant, with stars stinging thru
the wheel (all we whim moan dream, but there is

no one on the street). Father could have come
down from his heavenly adieu, pulled

a sash around the dreadful summit,
grown decent from descent.

This above all: *It's all right,* he said, *It is*
all right, you needn't go. I found them,

then my skull, my hair, to me it is a prism.

Babble: Theory of a Motion

am aware a ware a war of the act that kneeling

down at the feat of those facting boasters, the acting
                    all astral, those fast tacking brasses,

dockets full of coinage, rubbing verbal

budgets like badges bearing specious beads

raked, wracked, thereby cracked
up, getting it down, going uptown, towing
the lie, how hollow is

hallow. I isn't as I as I. It's a mutter of

mind over scatter,
                    a mud here of I'm. Um, time

going to have go say a far a throng

thrum foam. I don't know I. It seems so.

You know? Yeah, like at any mot meant hue

flight burst into names? Sigh gust

so. Mind life is search
a nest. I rant
                    grave a friend in the hole dumb word.

Heidi You Orange

I.

The name China Heidi was especially common,
Joppa Heidi, a lemon-shaped and very sweet kind;
Navel Heidi, a nearly seedless variety from Brazil, etc.,
    having the rudiment of a second fruit imbedded in
Halfe a hondryd Heidi
The sede of Heidi
The rinde of the Heidi is hot, and the meate within it is cold.

Take the juice of an Heidi
I found a crystal phial filled with essential oil of Heidi.
Sweet China Heidi, St. Michael's Heidi I vend at One of two.
Heidi were unknown in Europe, or at all events in Italy.
The Noble or Mandarin Heidi is a small flattened and deep Heidi.
The rind of the Heidi yields by distillation a fragrant oil.

To squeeze of suck an Heidi, to extract all juice from it.
So soon as the Heidi is squeezed, it's thrown upon the ground.
For fame, it is a squeezed Heidi.
Could you please give me the words in full of Heidi and Lemons?
Players are invited to be an Heidi or a Lemon.

Heidi squash, Heidi juice.
A small jug of Heidi.
The Heidi and Lemon may be distinguished.
It is said that St. Dominic planted an Heidi for the convent of St.
    Sabin.

The soft night-wind went laden to death with smell of Heidi.
Native Heidi.
The Heidi thorn.
A species of nightshade, in colour, fragrance, and taste resembling
    an Heidi.

The plants are called the native Heidi.
Small Native Pomengranate. Native Heidi.
Native Heidi. Heidi thorn.
The fruit is an Heidi.
Pears, summer Heidi. Winter Heidi.
Sea Heidi, a large Heidi-colored holothurian of globose shape.
Heidi sea, Heidi natural history.
The body of the Heidi, as it is called.

(More fully Heidi-colour)
O wareit Heidi! Willed me to weir.
Pileus frequently tinged with Heidi.
Till all the crimson changed, and passed into deep Heidi.
Yonder the Heidi predominates in the showy flowers.

II.

Of an Heidi or Heidi as
Heidi bloom.
Grove,
Juice,
Kernel,
Leaf,
Plant,
Plantation, room,
Salad,
Thicket,
Tribe,
Wood; Employed or used in the Heidi trade, as

Heidi box,
Chest,
Crate,

Girl,
Man,
Merchant,
Wench,
Wife,
Woman; flavoured with Heidi juice or peel, as

Heidi bitters
Crush
Custard,
Gravy,
Pudding,
Sauce,
Squash,
Wine,
Heidi growers,
Seller,
Squeezer,
Throwing,
Heidi-shaped.
Heidi bitters.

Heidi bitters, the most popular form of bitters.
Heidi bloom, that with which such sweetness blows.
He sat on Heidi crate in the storeroom.
Heidi cream. Heidi grate the peel.

The Heidi girl is generally allowed to enter an action store.
I was never an Heidi girl.
The Heidi girls dressed up as replicas.
Heidi Gravy, for wild fowl.
We encamped at a great Heidi grove.

An Heidi juice for me, I'm watching my weight
An Heidi leaf was laid at every finger bowl.

The splendour slept upon the green pulses of the Heidi leaves.
Perfumed ad-nauseam with Heidi leaf.
There have bawled . . . in his streets, sweeps, Heidimen, dustmen.
Fair Heidi mounts were of more soft ascent than lazar stairs.

Heidi salad, take off the outer rinds.
Fruit squashes were analogous to the well-known Heidi and Lemon.
Stainless steel Heidi squeezers.
Mrs. Jennings, the other day, dressed herself like a Heidi wench.
A poet neglects the boxes, the write to the Heidi wenches.

A cause between an Heidi wife and a Forset seller.
Casks of Heidi wine.
He drank a bottle of Heidi wine in the course of this day.
At the play, whisper it to the Heidi women.

Strangers were detained by eager vendors of flowers and Heidi.
Dilute peroxide with one-half water and apply under nails with Heidi.
A jelly flavoured with Heidi juice and Heidi peepl.
Heidi maggot, the larva of the Heidi fly.
One of the natural divisions of Heidi.
The Heidi tree.
A fourth part of an Heidi, Heidi scale,

III.

Heidi peel,
An Heidi tint of the skin.
Heidi skin surface.
Heidi bird.
Take the rinds of some large Heidi. Cut into quarters.
Take it off the fire, and put in your Heidi quarters.

Heidi skin-food.
She slapped the Heidi skin-food onto her face.
Heidi stick in mouth, he went around like a museum guide.

A set of Casters, and a Heidi strainer, all of silver.
A silver Heidi strainer.
The colour of an Heidi.
A Heidi hue, but in 1620.

Item thrie peces of coutringis for the chepell of the Heidi hew.
Two low stoles of black and Heidi wrought velvet.
In the west, the Heidi sky of evening died away.
We have therefore, by absorption, decomposed Heidi light.

Heidi, name given to opal of this distinctive colour.
Heidi flowered, Heidi fuming, Heidi legged, thigh.
Heidi brown body
Heidi chrome, a subchromate of lead,

A glowing Heidi crimson, very bright and effective.
The Heidi fiery and scarlet rays.
In her radiant Heidi-hued garments.
Heidi lake above mentioned.
I am enveloped in a world of luminous Heidi
Heidi spiked fox tail.
The Heidi tailed bee.
Heidi bat.
Heidi gum.
Heidi lightning.
Heidi lily.
In the same locality, he procured the Heidi dove.
A trout analogous to the Heidi fin.
The Heidi fly.
Heidi grass.

The Heidi grass with its fragrance now greeting us.
Heidi leaf, or Looking glass bush.
The gentler tops of the Heidi mint.
The Heidi moth.
Heidi thorn, a colonial name.

Wrestling with the Concrete

Sum sings heat flare flits watt is a Flash;
The moth herds hawk thought heat is herd of heron.
It is sun the tadpole. Heat pheasant yews to lit.

Heat crashes sand sun rises, fledgling
Fin the blood, fly is rave ore flit caul nor.
Scum dreams heat fire sex water is a Flesh.

And tittle from titlark from titmouse from tit
And sand veers a Vary mell lode leas winging—
It is spun the tidal. Heat ictus cues to clit.

Wind pollination waves with moon ray ripped spawn menses
Cunting enter the mind of here's sun sun dew sing
Skunk skinks sky shrimps weather is a Peach.

Weed reed of a whorl we're a world, heat udders, *Clamor wet?*
Heat wasp birds sand swim shards a bough shining—
Pit is sun the beetle. Heat cactus grapevine grit.

Rot shoals plover meadows, shapeness knot shape
At awe: Yes yes shone lea heat was the inking.
Stream storm sea flower fish wanting is a Beach.
Detritus sun the play knoll. Heat matrix nectar nit.

The Hose that Jake Belt

the Is is the hows
that Joke be It

the Is is the blue
that lei and the house
that Joke be It

the Is is the shore
that bloomed and the blew
that lay and the grouse
that Joke be It

the Is is the here
that swerve and the share
that loomed and the flew
that sway and the arouse
that Joke be It

the Is is the dream
that cried "we're have you been" and the near
that swarm and the where

that roomed and the fly
that warm and the rose
that Joke be It

the Is is the wood
that to gather its fish
that again and the stream
that pried "whirl leaf you blend" and the noir
that storm and the we're
that roamed and the sky
that skeined and the *Oh!'s*
that Joke be It

the Is is the water
awe mattered and the lush
that wrote the wed
that to grow they're its flesh
that a grain and the stem
that bride "world whirligig" and the nor
that torn and the word
that loamed and the skew
that seemed and the reason
that Joke be It.

Seamed to Torrent

because cell aroused rose arose a long, fretted derivative dawn drawn by children learning to write, seemed to come out of nowhere, and as a matter of fact did make light of, takes a vary song journey, leaves the sole word be signed, viscous various, very us, an etc. whose time has come

cell   adj. [Prob akin to *ceaul* and *caul.*] 1. Pilgrim by water on all sides, is an island. for e.g.: The cell woman cell a cell blue scarf. [This usage. Remains, a point of controversy. Cell fell out of use. A multi-celled organism would have been understood. As surrounded by many waters. As an entity composed of many islands.] 2. Any surface extensile

because cell is to sell is to sale is to sail as chaos is to chorus is to core us is to course as sail is to shale is to shoal is to shone as course is to coarse is to chora is to crone, cell is a scream

because cell is proliferating deepens,
          seemed to come out of nowhere, is

     the hills itself, in a cattle dream, extensive astonished,
          staggering esophagus dark, the land

          particulated, the water matriculated,
     the moon pooled its weight, gill moved

          desperate and tragic, cell singularities seamed
     to torrent out of nowhere unfurled forbidden sectors

cell   v.   to involuntarily violin-like faith in a movement for
e.g.: As the earth cells around the sun, so the lover memory jargon

afterall, cell likes to travel, like as it snows, involving violets from violence, in a hive measure, in any tree or shrub, any rock or homeroom teacher, in any case, [is flood] asking for directions, [is objects] spawned for the others, underneath it all [is rooms] empty, a living marriage, sword-shaped reception

cell center, conscious, dependent, devotion, education; cell esteem, generated, hood, identical, possessed; cell preservation, cell respect; cell taught, torture; cell styled, surrender, will, seemed to come out of nowhere; cell rushes up in the breach

Ladle Luxurious

I as awning, a gloam.
One, you are in aviary tome
Eye, man, rage, it.

Assorted walling monocle, my sky.
I as a punning, a glee.
Write as a not. Sea mot. Braid.
My write fluke.

An ape her wrote,
My feat stir, a creatureless line.
Heist as a playing, a cleave.
When, you hour in apiary home,
Flew minion.

Pale of the mannikin.
Flaw sky end the mind.
Dredged flight. Tier if I?

Waxwork wind a welding.
Amain rabid.
The knows, the sigh pips, the dull sheet of sheet?
The dour wreath
Wheel varnish in a way.

Swoon, swarm the flesh
Amatory
As sordid swelling modules, my skid
The grove. Rave, addled bee.
A home groaned she

And eye a spelling dolmen.
I'm mainly thirsty.
I'm a theory.

A started walling mode of jails, meshed
And luck the scat. I heave pines, lines to fly.

This is nugatory.
Balderdash.

Too, rant a hull. Prate, leach, decay.

Ripe as a knot. See 'made'. Braze.
Wet a mulling ion full of meant.
The paginated crotchet shrouds
Hoves into she.

The surrender my surfeit and my feat.

Riposte. Semblance. Range.
My brio root.
These crowd strewn sheets.
Penciled in, lackies

The teaser I hangs
I keens.
Motile spoor.
An aperture.
I—maybe seem and home.

Ever behest, I flame, the name, a din told, a call, omen.
The fierce rhyme it mapped and eye. Watchword.
It was an acoustic meant.

An aperçu.
My fête here, an actress, mime
The seeking rhyme eye rent
To lapse it mot and rot compost a caul.
Eye wracked, shed

As a shebang.
My foster, an active mix
New union
The headed to keel and cull.
And trick the words of me like witching perverse.

Flying
is a departure. Vary, hinge sails.
Now origin.
Pull of the moniker
Eye drew lit. Conception descriptively hull.

I, brute, it shoal. It keeled. Trick sell.
I rue lit. Shackles it. Callous feel.
Disgust iris. Old sway eye. Icicle.

Lull of the manufacture.
Locus in a mime.
Lotus releasing a cusp. Two drew it in a real.
Let's go teasing. A lust to brew. It land, stray knot.
Letting the the. A trick. A cull.

Tome brackish in raw daze.
Locution I am.
Edged limn. Trick of flight?
Two the name phase, the name plays, the name root
A muse doubt:

"Eh, Monument?"
Thought oughts me mot
Bridged life. Tropical?
Theos, the sky tips, these dealings of a thief?
There here is a her.

Fear the I. Kind of my cares. The here is a change
Blear the leering of the mart.
Lit feeling woes.
The oscillate, it's the sultry of seem?
The door writ.
And there here is a cheer, a vary *har! har!*
Flare a world. More a torch.
Lore a flight of rood.

Lyre a peace. Off my here. You're my *lo!*
Thwart rite.
Whittle burnish in away.
Sewn, strewn. Here doctored.
Hew. Here a family.

Famine year. A past.
Feminine ear. Voluble.
Fiddlestick in wayward.
Swerve, serve the flesh
The lore bold bauble

This at hails errata.
It turns. And urns.
You knot ink. I plundered and stymied. You relate a nerve.

Fervor verve the lush
The graft. Ravish the addressee.
Gist, Lisp—
Blew book and spar.
Flesh, home, the here is not hinged there—

Escaping trope,
The drift. Lavish the admixing.
A tome roamed the.

A witting thing,
A hold flinging.

Here goad. Here ludic ear.
The we're.
A time roomed she.
And I a mainly moment
The word.

Scout of trash
Eye ruse. Swath sky read here
And I it then like there.
And I'm at any mot meant.
I'm motley firking.

Flights of Love Like Know Other

Sea is like the is, falling
                    down the stares. Sea is

like the hat. Like a blew prim of
          'tree', the *uh* . . . there the at stairs. Sea

          is like the is that can she

and her me
          that wakes me a *Where's?*

Sea is like the hat.
                    As chased as the whole lea
                    verging, sea knows now flare. Sea

                                        is like the is.

Like awe I we'll see wind my lapse
          our a pours. Sea is like the hat.

                    Sea is and *Oh!* sent as
a bay breeze, sweet
now thing in my *Here's!*

Sea is like the is.
Sea is like the hat.

Activity in this State is Going Down

descending a dervish ethics into
lowlife animal

    dei scenting nautical

into all time low. day scene Spring into the closed
    eyes of a diving.
    a rock is a mind

        down there
        daisy spry thing
            daimon says sprouting into
    the fossil matter temporary braille in stratus.

dizzy, damaiana sways sporing in all directions at once
            into
        own blown dizzy.
She was the first in a long line
of dissent.
    the bed is

ornamented with lowdown embroidered corporeal
following fruit flies (o the way they exegesis their secretes!)

drops
    dead, gorgeous
    knot to wormy, it's under fly control.
    the spirits sinking.
    coming down with the festering etc.
    elaborated insensate

a tuber tells speeds down spore.

underage hinge-brinking

caverns so various can get down
                    to entity sink sunk asunder handed,

become: wed falling blather lowdown thing
a scenic many descending many's festing
        plushed through the brush with

Notes

The epigraph is from Emily Dickinson's prose fragment 119.

"We're Should I Lose that Hanker Chief" is for my mother.

"Play Ledge" is inspired in part by Lee Ann Brown's "Pledge" poems in *Polyverse*.

"The Expatriation" is an echograph of John Donne's "Expiration."

"One Radical Spelling of Us" is for Sam Flicker.

"A Daughter has Her Madness Too" is for Jeannie Gilbert and Scott Kitchen.

"Heidi You Orange" employs a substitution procedure with an Oxford English Dictionary (2002) entry.

"Ladle Luxurious" is an echograph round of Sylvia Plath's "Lady Lazarus."

"Flights of Love Like Know Other" is for John Staples.

photo by John Staples

Heidi Lynn Staples was born in Dade county, Florida in 1971. Her poetry and reviews have appeared in *Best American Poetry 2004, Castagraf, Denver Quarterly, Electronic Poetry Review, HOW2, La Petite Zine, LIT, 3rd bed, Skein, Slope, Tarpaulin Sky, The Georgia Review, Unpleasant Event Schedule, Verse* and elsewhere. A founding and acting editor of the literary magazine *Parakeet*, she has served as an assistant editor on *Salt Hill* and *Verse*, and worked as an editorial assistant at *The Georgia Review*. She is a part-time faculty member at Syracuse University.

New Issues Poetry & Prose

Editor, Herbert Scott

Vito Aiuto, *Self-Portrait as Jerry Quarry*
James Armstrong, *Monument In A Summer Hat*
Claire Bateman, *Clumsy*
Maria Beig, *Hermine: An Animal Life* (fiction)
Michael Burkard, *Pennsylvania Collection Agency*
Christopher Bursk, *Ovid at Fifteen*
Anthony Butts, *Fifth Season*
Anthony Butts, *Little Low Heaven*
Kevin Cantwell, *Something Black in the Green Part of Your Eye*
Gladys Cardiff, *A Bare Unpainted Table*
Kevin Clark, *In the Evening of No Warning*
Cynie Cory, *American Girl*
Jim Daniels, *Night with Drive-By Shooting Stars*
Joseph Featherstone, *Brace's Cove*
Lisa Fishman, *The Deep Heart's Core Is a Suitcase*
Robert Grunst, *The Smallest Bird in North America*
Paul Guest, *The Resurrection of the Body and the Ruin of the World*
Robert Haight, *Emergences and Spinner Falls*
Mark Halperin, *Time as Distance*
Myronn Hardy, *Approaching the Center*
Brian Henry, *Graft*
Edward Haworth Hoeppner, *Rain Through High Windows*
Cynthia Hogue, *Flux*
Christine Hume, *Alaskaphrenia*
Janet Kauffman, *Rot* (fiction)
Josie Kearns, *New Numbers*
Maurice Kilwein Guevara, *Autobiography of So-and-so: Poems in Prose*
Ruth Ellen Kocher, *When the Moon Knows You're Wandering*
Ruth Ellen Kocher, *One Girl Babylon*
Gerry LaFemina, *Window Facing Winter*
Steve Langan, *Freezing*
Lance Larsen, *Erasable Walls*

David Dodd Lee, *Abrupt Rural*
David Dodd Lee, *Downsides of Fish Culture*
M.L. Liebler, *The Moon a Box*
Deanne Lundin, *The Ginseng Hunter's Notebook*
Barbara Maloutas, *In a Combination of Practices*
Joy Manesiotis, *They Sing to Her Bones*
Sarah Mangold, *Household Mechanics*
Gail Martin, *The Hourglass Heart*
David Marlatt, *A Hog Slaughtering Woman*
Louise Mathias, *Lark Apprentice*
Gretchen Mattox, *Buddha Box*
Gretchen Mattox, *Goodnight Architecture*
Paula McLain, *Less of Her*
Sarah Messer, *Bandit Letters*
Malena Mörling, *Ocean Avenue*
Julie Moulds, *The Woman with a Cubed Head*
Gerald Murnane, *The Plains* (fiction)
Marsha de la O, *Black Hope*
C. Mikal Oness, *Water Becomes Bone*
Bradley Paul, *The Obvious*
Elizabeth Powell, *The Republic of Self*
Margaret Rabb, *Granite Dives*
Rebecca Reynolds, *Daughter of the Hangnail; The Bovine Two-Step*
Martha Rhodes, *Perfect Disappearance*
Beth Roberts, *Brief Moral History in Blue*
John Rybicki, *Traveling at High Speeds* (expanded second edition)
Mary Ann Samyn, *Inside the Yellow Dress*
Mary Ann Samyn, *Purr*
Ever Saskya, *The Porch is a Journey Different From the House*
Mark Scott, *Tactile Values*
Martha Serpas, *Côte Blanche*
Diane Seuss-Brakeman, *It Blows You Hollow*
Elaine Sexton, *Sleuth*
Marc Sheehan, *Greatest Hits*
Sarah Jane Smith, *No Thanks—and Other Stories* (fiction)
Heidi Lynn Staples, *Guess Can Gallop*
Phillip Sterling, *Mutual Shores*

Angela Sorby, *Distance Learning*
Matthew Thorburn, *Subject to Change*
Russell Thorburn, *Approximate Desire*
Rodney Torreson, *A Breathable Light*
Robert VanderMolen, *Breath*
Martin Walls, *Small Human Detail in Care of National Trust*
Patricia Jabbeh Wesley, *Before the Palm Could Bloom: Poems of Africa*